WINTER WITH FLOWERS

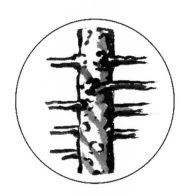

James Clarke

HLC Press

Guelph, Ontario

ISBN: (pbk) 978-1-928171-29-4
ISBN: (ebk) 978-1-928171-30-0

Press

Guelph, Ontario

For Kathy & our families
Omnia vincit amor

ACKNOWLEDGMENTS

I am indebted to my daughter Marilyn Clarke for the cover image, to my grandson James Clarke-Hicks for the emblem, to my daughter-in-law Carrie McClary for her editing, and to my friend Jeremy Luke Hill for the cover design and typesetting.

An old man loved is winter with flowers.
— German Proverb

WINTER WITH FLOWERS

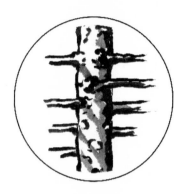

James Clarke

Friend, I write these poems
For you, small mirrors to breathe
Upon & wipe away the haze to
Better see the original face you
Were born with, the one that will
Survive all your challenging moods &
Masks, be with you in the end.

GRACE NOTES

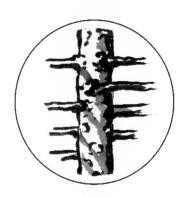

SPRING INCANTATION

Put away the dank
            wool of winter;
let sun thaw
            the hard bud,
erase old grooves
            of thinking.

Let spring begin
            its green tribute to
bourgeoning life,
            clean soiled hands
with new rain.
            Bless & be blest.

INSATIABLE QUEST

This morning a muffled drumbeat against the
      bedroom window wakened me.

Outside, a robin, feathers askew & wobbly,
      teetered on a branch trying

to catch his balance. The windowpane reflected
      back his orange vest, wet

green stalks of trees & milk-blue sky. That
      morning & the next & next

the bird thumped against the glass, each time
      knocked back by the

same invisible wall, ruffled & shaken, till at last
      it dawned on me that it would

never give up; like us, caged in skin, who long
      to beat our way heavenward,

he'd keep trying to break free, enter that dim
      lush paradise, prepared

if need be, to go on forever.

ONE BLESSING AT A TIME

The moon's radiance has dimmed. This story
you tell me has no stars in it. Keep alert —listen—
this darkness has no bad intentions. At this very
hour someone you scarcely know reaches
out, whispers your name. Put your trust
in the hands of the god of small blessings.

SUNSET

Another evening drawing in
across the lake as we gather
by the window to see the spent
sun burning deep inside the
trees, cottage wall aflame.
Compassed by doubt & dark I
try to cup the dancing fire.
"Shame it doesn't stay," I say,

forgetting in my heart's desire
that someone, somewhere on this
turning globe, is always catching
gold, the dazzling coin spinning
from eye to eye, the air beyond
our darkening hands holier than rain.

HEART'S NEEDLE

Last evening

as darkness thickened I walked down to the
lake to listen to the

thrum of raindrops, watch the ripples flatten &
fade, a break of moonlight

on the darkish sand. Slowly, slowly
I am learning to unclench my hand.

ALL SUMMER LONG
— *for Palma*

I

Last fall my old aunt was in hospital
dying of cancer, or so we thought;
she won't walk again, the doctor
said, gave her six months to live.

"Doesn't he know our family's hard
to kill, "she said, but saw
the notary just in case, made a will,
signed a contract for her burial.

Her only wish, she said, was to swim
her mountain lake, one last time.

II

Now summer's here, she's fooled us all,
totters to the shore on bone-white legs,
slides off the dock into the green dark lake
and pushes out. She has no fear, moves

with natural grace, floats on her back (you
must trust the water to hold you up
she says). All summer long she swims—
each day, one last time—closes her eyes
and lets the sun caress her face, swims
across the bay & back: "I could swim forever."

SPIRIT HOUSE

Like water
through the bottom
of an old pail

or sunlight
through a torn
black coat

it catches me
by surprise,
my heart stalls,

I step out
of my body,
break into wings,

whirl
above the tips
of evergreens

till I ache
to touch
the bright, descending roof,

those nights
at Limerick Lake
when stars come out.

HOLY VOICES

I emerge from the dark womb of
      sleep, step into the stillness
of a Sunday morning, my feet
      wet & shining from the
cold night dew, imagine I hear the
      breath of grass awakening,
a brush of a Monarch's wing amongst
      the flowers, the small,
sweet trill of a sparrow on a fence,
      sabbath notes hinged between
two worlds, whispers from
      the far side of silence.

UNEXPECTED MERCIES

There are small gifts that I forget
to give thanks for; they drop from

aloft, unbidden & unseen — like the
Monarchs this morning in my yard

that descended from the green canopy
of leaves & for a few brief moments

frisked in the sombre air around me,
startled my jaded mind with wonder.

BENEDICTIONS

Sometimes when the world breaks over you
like a dark wave, distills the last small drop
of hope within your veins & baffled, you no
longer know where to turn or how to pray,-

a sudden gift: bubbles of light on the ribbed
hull of a gold leaf along your way; a marsh
hawk, poised & imperious, white rump on
pole in the belly of a bush, kee kee keeing into

the cool & colourless air; or on a bare fall night
furred with frost & just beyond your windowsill
a spill of stars, brilliant as the eyes of children,
earth's sweet-tongued orisons that nudge you

out of self, unlatch the chamber of your cold-
dumb heart, utter your own unspoken prayer.

EPIPHANY

A snowshoe hare
           caught me by surprise
this morning,
           paused in a webwork of light
on my shadowy path
           just long enough
to chew a clover leaf,
           flick its tawny ears,
send me a sidelong incurious glance &
           disappear,

but not before leaving
           a shining in the grass
so dazzling that, wide-eyed,
           I fell skyward,
a tapered blue sky
           folding round my heart.

RANDOM GRACES

Even when weather turns cruel,
the light hard & brittle, everyone
locked in bleak winter thoughts,
shivering in their bones, unexpected
moments of grace appear —
children on the sidewalk,
heads tilted to gaze at eaves
of dripping ice needles, their
curious eyes startled by
the cold splash of wonder

THERE ARE DAYS

I wake with the rising sun,
        peace brimming my heart —
no need for the distorted logic of
        memory or a new moon
to bring good news, lift me out of
        self-defeating ways.

I lay back & contemplate the light
        streaming through my window,
content to listen, patient as a stone,
        to early birds gossiping
among themselves, the silver music
        of birches, small reminders
of all I can never be dispossessed.

OH HOW I WISH IT SO

morning tips
        the dish of night
spills her beads
        of blue and rose and white;
last night
        I rode the dragon of sleep
across the long ocean
        deep into
your watery cave
        watched you rise
unfold your glassy wings
        and say:
all all is light

O how I wish it so

POET'S HAVEN

*"Who would have thought my shrivelled
heart could have recorded greenness."*
— George Herbert

And now in winter,

      after such dire depletion,

with so many fires

      banked,

this dry wood

      rekindles

my green words,

      sleep's little darkness

folding into

      amazing light.

RESURRECTION

Last January,
               when the ice storm
sheathed the earth in glass
               the spindly spruce
at the front of the house
               bent its stiff bones
across the roadway,
               doomed.

Now after the tooth & tomb of winter,
               surprise!
new eyes flickering
               in green amazement
from every twig.

ARRIVAL OF SPRING

Outside: winter —
        unending waves
of dismal days;
        the maple outside
the back window, —
        a black fish
skeleton.

Then, suddenly this
        morning, skeins of
seaweed
        snagged
on every bone —
        the sweeping rush
of green.

REVEILLE

Time to rise & take to the road.

In this inexhaustible light, I forget
gaudy figurines & dark voices, the
stealthy passing of the night. The hour
is now — the artist within yearns to
be elsewhere — follow the arcing sun.

MESSAGE IN A BOTTLE

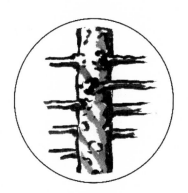

ANOTHER SWIM

He plunges into the lake,
almost alone — loons rehearse
their long flight south.

On the far shore,
red & gold maples.

A neighbour has told him
he's foolish to swim
so late in the season.

He wants to tell
his neighbour: no one escapes
the bondage of dead dreams.

He is not deaf
to autumnal whispers:
Swim as far as you can.

THE ART OF CANOEING
— for John Hicks

requires quiet hands,
hands that hear
the music
of the paddle,

hold the wood
of the world gently.

UNDERCOAT
— for Paul

My son, the teacher who's helping me paint
the four Victorian-style screen doors I

bought for the cottage, knows my habits better
than myself, spreads papers on the deck where

I'll be working, tells me to leave spindles, ginger-
bread, the wood around the knobs for him.

"And don't load up your brush," he says. "Remember,
less is more." We divide the paint (premium quality

primer—"the best always lasts") & go about our separate
tasks but not before he chides me to slow down.

"Life's too short," he says. I watch him kneeling by
the bunky door below, Bach's Magnificat

on the radio; he doesn't slap on paint like me; his
strokes are soft & sure, caress the wood; occasionally

he stops, inspects his work, retouches—the epitome
of mindfulness. "Painting's a form of meditation,"

he loves to say. Afterwards he looks at my flecked
face & skin, shows me his clean hands & grins.

SLOUCHING TOWARD TOMORROW

Sometimes we feel like
        orphans of light, powerless be-
fore the jagged debris of
        a broken world. Sometimes we
stand at a crossroads under
        a darkening sky that no longer
whispers of infinite stars,
        baffled how we became so lost,
whether we will ever recover
        those crude maps of thinking
locked with all our good
        intentions in caves of memor-
abilia. But just when all
        seems black, our path in doubt,
nothing between us & the
        latched windows of heaven, an
inner voice impels us to
        question the brute force of dark-
ness, search again for that
        one small curl of redeeming fire —
the herald of a new tomorrow.

THE SCARY THING

is you can say anything:

that the diamond solitaire just below the place
you love to be kissed will slow your breathing;

that all you need for happiness is an island where
the pulse slows in time to the undulating waves &
you can hear the song of the kisadee miles away;

that those shiny appliances will take the frazzle
out of your marriage;

that the revolutionary skin serum with 8% Mexican yam will
soothe the torrential inner sanctum of your body & give you peace;

that this new seductive perfume will make you drop your
broom & raise hell;

that the line between sensuality & safety no longer
exists in your automobile;

that your garden will be the talk of the beehive,

and someone will believe you.

A POET'S WORK

Burn the dead wood of
platitudes in the fired
language of poetry.

The poet climbs the
slender stem of poetry
to reach the healing sun.

My shadow and I
meet briefly on the written
page and then pass on.

Doing dishes, the
poet soaks his wordy mind
in sudsy water.

Stiff and stone deaf he
is far from dead—listens to
haikus in his head.

MESSAGE IN A BOTTLE

A man walks along a sea shore, with the usual miscellany of gauzy thoughts that pass for reflection, amidst a litter of sea-weed and rotten wood, crushed cans and dead fish. He comes upon a green-tinted bottle, sees a paper inside. Curious, he picks it up, manages to get the paper out & discovers it's a message: *Ever since I got stranded on the island I've longed to connect with you. What is your name? Where do you live? Are you happy? Solitude can be a crock, agreed? Did I tell you about my stroll on the beach one evening? I was looking at the scarlet sleeve of sky when night sprang up, a sheet of starlight above my head. It's so beautiful here I never want to leave. Sometimes I think I'm talking to the dead, but send my messages anyway. It's the only way I know to find you.*

The man slowly folds the paper, gazes out at the sea for a long time, his head swirling with questions.

PLEASE WRITE SOON

I love letters spun from the transparent
fibres of the heart: nothing stimulates

me more than the flutter of mail pushing
through the slot like moths. I keep

them close at hand, the way a flamenco
dancer holds a fan, change continents

just to fondle their delicate frames. Today
alas, bills, notices, circulars by the

score, but letters scarcely any more,
faded like ghostly silhouettes on

a darkened screen; even letters to get
letters are of no avail; intimacy travels

so swiftly these days my news is always
stale; friends tell me when I complain

that I must get e-mail. O for the bloom
of handwriting on a page — the porous

human smudge! A perfect printout is never
quite the same. Please write soon.

EASTER WEEK IN PALM SPRINGS
— after Heather King

The sun still glitters in the aging palm trees of this desert
oasis.

Downtown an effigy of a young Marilyn Monroe pays
homage to the dreams of its tanned denizens.

Odometers strapped to their arms, octogenarians shuffle
on varicose-veined legs toward the health spas;

in the casinos, the pfft, pfft, of breathing machines whisper:
"keep playing, you never know, this could be your big day;"

round the private golf Club a doughty scraggle of retirees
wends its way, gazes into the dim distance for the next
green, praying for one last lucky shot,

the Resurrection, at the end of the course, a wavering hope.

GRACE OF THE ORDINARY

All over the globe this Christmas
people are foraging in the big box

stores for the latest Specials: cut-
ting-edge smart phones; magic

breadmaker, or that marvelous
self-levitation machine everyone's

been raving about, anything more
novel & promising than being down

here in Basement Household far from
tinselly shelves, celebrating old

rituals with family & friends amidst
dishcloths, brooms, plain flatware &

wooden tables, learning to feed each
other's deepest hungers with

everyday spoons

FIVE WISHES
— after Anne Porter

I'd like to cradle the passenger
Pigeon in my arms, stroke
Its long rosy neck
Slender blue-black tail
Feel   just once
Its red beating heart

I'd like to see once more
Milne's watercolours of the
Country north of Bancroft
The hills & lakes
                 I love

Baptiste on the cusp of
Morning   the white horn
Of driftwood curving
                 into waters
Still as stone

And I would like to go back to
Trosly-Breuil wander alone
In the evening
The winding lanes past
                the red roofed houses
Of yellow stone   smell
The green damp of the Compiègne forest
And the small chapel
In the village square   the Virgin
In the upper window
       In blue & white.

And I would like to learn
The art of loving
—the holy longing of the wise—
Before I go

Enter the narrow gate
That even God Himself
Could not open
       for us.

And I would like to visit Ars
In the Massif Central
Where the simple curé worked his wonders
And pilgrims still come with
       crutches & canes
To hang their broken hearts.

I'd love to go there
With my beloved

And it would be enough
Just being there

MY ONE ALLOTTED QUESTION

Lord,
by what whimsy of divine justice
did you allow
a man disposed to evasion
who sees but
dimly through the shadows
to sit on a glass throne
judging others?

TURNING 80

Showers abbreviate the air
on this third ring of the sun;
a cloud-capped arch morphs
into a rainbow.

As the speed of life confounds me, I teach
my grey heart to sing: go slow, go slow, go slow,
and learn to inhale, exhale
in the blazing Now of this, our once-only,
gratitude — a blessing white as vapour
on my breath.

Each day, the last day.

EASTER

All night,
clinking of glass,
      dad reeling off
all the books
of the Old Testament
in a blurry voice,
laughter,
song,
arguments and tears.

Daybreak,
everyone asleep
      the stench
of beer and nicotine
in the room,
kitchen bristling
          with
broken glass,
empty bottles,
butt burns and ash
on oil cloth,
tenement quiet as a tomb.

Dark undone,
bells announce
the coming of the sun,
 roadway,
  windows,
   trees
    catch fire,
me — Adam
on the first blond day,
spinning
in new-born light.

UNREAD MEMOIR

The morning of the operation I told my sister
in the hospital that I'd just finished a memoir
of our chaotic childhood. I didn't want her to
be alarmed when she read it & found that my
memory of what happened differed from hers.
"There's no single version of a shared past,"
I told her. "You know, Dad's a ghost to me now"
she said. "Maybe your account of our child-
hood will bring back some of the good things
I've forgotten."

For a long moment we held hands in silence.
When the orderlies finally came and wheeled
her down the empty corridor, she raised her
hand to her lips, smiled & blew me a kiss. "I
love you, too," I whispered in her direction.
Then the stainless steel doors swung open
& she disappeared from view, slipping quietly
into a timeless Now where none of our memoirs
are unread, nothing's forgotten or unsaid.

WALKING THE CORPSE HOME

The old poet, lost within himself, is walking
home backwards as they say in China. He has

assigned himself the hard work of memory,
refuses to die on some dusty road in a foreign

land far away from his hearth. Alert to the
hungry ghosts within him, he rises early to

track the morning sun, revisits old haunts &
hurts, determined to make amends for all the

defections & missteps of the first half of life
when he was too callow & mindless to pay

attention. He is walking backwards to find
himself, living his life twice. He is going home.

HOW STRANGE

we starry-eyed wayfarers
      married to the haunts & habits of
transient corporal vessels,
      journeying through night-fouled
seas toward a veiled, ever receding horizon,
      searching in all the wrong places for
a permanence that outlasts us all —
      a safe harbour & haven, to know
at last what it is to arrive.

STRUGGLING TO SING WITH ANGELS

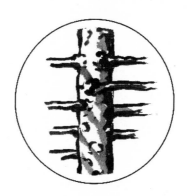

DREAM CATCHER

I stumbled
> through the nerve ends
of many winters,
> lost & disoriented till
I met you, vowed
> never to be lost again.

Yet here I am,
> years after you disappeared,
sitting by a window where
> no birds sing, wrapped
in solitude, still longing
> for a new spring, —
the promise of
> a journey home.

ON READING MILOSZ

You wrote that even memory is under sentence
of death, described how the pitiless waters will

close over all of us, both living & dead, erase our
names & memories, every single, brilliant

moment that made our lives vivid & unique,
washed away into a Lethian netherworld as

though it was all a cruel jest. Your grim
prediction made me shudder. Tell me it isn't so,

Czeslaw. Where did the music go?
Where did it come from?

I need to know, I need to know.

THE FIRE

In the dream he walked across a field
under the palest, silken blue, past

the tall sweet corn, all the way to
the big pond where he dug a trench, circled

it with rocks, gathered bark, wood shavings,
twigs, coniferous seed cones, dead

wood, branches for fuel; then, as dusk
descended & fireflies came out he

built a pyre that lit up pond & sky, &
wife, child, mother, father, sister, grand-

parents, relatives, old friends, none dead,
none absent, joined him at the fire,

dark faces polished with love, no one
speaking, as though everyone was seeing

each other for the first time, shriven &
accepted as they'd always dreamed, eyes

picked clean by the long patience of death.

VIGIL

After she left
        he drifted through
endless corridors of
        winter, past the room
where her face ought to be,
        nerve ends frayed, stars
hidden from sight
        behind banks of apathy &
fatigue, yearning
        for a new spring, the
promise of a journey home.

Twenty years later
        he's still waiting for that
curl of clear, green light.

SILVER MERCIES

"It takes seven years for a suicide,"
the priest said, but I was too numb

to hear his words: that was when the black
spring of tongues of tulips pierced my

heart and the thought of never seeing
her again was more than I could bear.

Last night when her long beautiful
arms reached across the bed, huge with

desire, and I could not even remember her
voice, that rich resonance that once filled

our home with warmth and joy, I grieved for
all our faithless flesh too small for

even strongest love; but snow,
our comforter, knows us better than

ourselves and covers us whitely, seven
times seven, with soft forgetfulness, and

just as the hibiscus never completely fades
but rises red and radiant always

in our mind, so too the snowy voices
of those we loved live in our reborning

selves, silver mercies of the dead.

PERMANENCE
— for Amelia

After the funeral my granddaughter whispered in her
mother's ear: "I want to be alone with papa," &
so I took her by the hand, led
her into the living room, thinking
we could have a quiet time together.
She leaned the slight weight
of her four-year-old head against my chest, nestled
in my arms, mute & still & safe &

for the longest while we held each other—our
hearts, two shells resonating in the dark—
the wet, white seconds like lanterns soaking up
the night, her life-breath—a small urgent bell
making me promise over & over I would never leave.

WINTER PRAYER

The arc of my sun is turning downwards.
Confounded by the cold finality of death
my heart has been shorn of its thin armour,
shudders, naked & vulnerable, before the
ebbing of warmth. I cannot accept that the
light in the countenances of those I knew & loved —
spun out of ageless star furnaces & DNA
mutations — should flare up briefly only to
disappear forever. Lord help my unbelief,
guide me through this dream-like blur of
days. I am not resigned.

WINTER SOLSTICE

I grieve the cold, trackless
stars, the shadows, sharply

bent and harsh against the snow;
wind in trees outside my window

moves like someone passing. Moon
is full—a large pearly bulge; no

telescope can explain its cool
back-lit glow; the earth

tilts on its axis, flies elliptically
around the sun but even

on darkest days the sun stands
still; it is we who leave.

The lamp in my kitchen is not
strong enough to

pierce the dark, the weight of
absence presses against

the glass. I've decided to
burn a candle, however

brief, await the slow unfettered
light of dawn, let

memory sweeten grief.

UNEXPECTED CONSOLATION

Death barged in on me one day,
sealed me behind an icy wall of silence,
with no one to cling to or console me, but
the Forsaken One, who drew me into the
shadow of His cross, held me in the
stillness of his grieving arms.

TO CARRY DEATH

Sometimes I carry death
       in my arms;
often she's closer to me
       than my bones.

Sometimes I go outside
       peer into smoke-
coloured clouds,
       the colour of desperation,
hoping to glimpse
       the bright promises
of heaven.

How could I
       have ever imagined
I would stray so far,
       be kept waiting
so long
       in this blizzard
of Eden.

WHEN THE DEAD ARE STILL NEAR

In the wilderness of grieving — a trackless
wasteland of thorns and sinkholes—the
dead visit our solitude, whisper to us
from the other side of silence.

Take comfort from their companionship.
Wait in silence for what their voices, still
near, tell us.

The words of the dead strike sparks from
stones, light the path we all must follow.

ETTY'S PRAYER

Bid farewell to all prescriptions, worries,
Slogans, any conventional bulwarks;
Put your papers in order; safe in His
Arms, let your loves go free.

Clear out the debris, the non-essential
That blocks the thinking heart. Abandon
Words such as "god" "death" "suffering,"
Become as simple & wordless as the

Growing corn or falling rain; let your life
Overflow in a constant stream of tenderness,
Eternity seep into every cranny of your day;
Learn to kneel; even in the face of death

Give praise; become as a little bird tucked
Away in His protective hand.

VILLANELLE

I find it hard to say goodbye,
blooms must bow before the rain.
We are in love with things that die.

The sun that warms my waking eye
too soon is gone, like every Dick and Jane
I find it hard to say goodbye.

Clouds that prance across the sky
all day, by dusk are tumbled slain.
We are in love with things that die.

We sacrifice our temple doves to buy
a little time, but all in vain.
I find it hard to say goodbye.

Our loves like leaves unhook and fly,
there is no greening for our pain.
We are in love with things that die.

Who made the heart to hurl so high
if fall it must to dust again?
I find it hard to say goodbye.
We are in love with things that die.

THE YEARNING

This spring for the first time in thirty
        years buds didn't appear on the paper

birch in the crevice of the rock by the shore.
        Last summer it quaked like a young bride

in the breeze, swallows nested in the thick
        dazzle of its green hair. Every April

it's worn the same hard appearance of death,
        the empty spaces like the terrible longing

between people, but that never stopped its
        soft fluent growth—the green-tipped nubbins,

then the pale yellow petals unfolding from
        every twig. "The buds are always late,"

I say, touching a bare branch. My daughter
        Ruth thinks I'm in denial. "Give up, Dad,

no one's coming back," she says. I kneel
on the rock, numbstruck, unwilling to disbelieve,

        wondering how long I'll have to wait.

STRAY DEVOTIONS

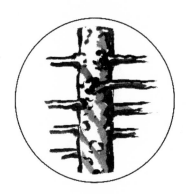

THE HEALER

He touched the sick,
prayed in tongues,
scoured the Book of the One
whose name is
Unearthed Lightening.

"Divinity's a mountain
behind the mind," he said.

THE STEEPLE
— for Father Kevin

I climbed to the top
      of the old stone church,
sneaked up the staircase
      to the choir loft, ascended
the ladder to the windy belfry;
      steeple swayed,
splinters scratched my face,
      nails tore my clothes
as I groped skyward
      into that narrowing space,
darkness round me closing
      like a trap,
fearful, perhaps I had gone too far,
      till at last I bumped my head
against the Cross,
      discovered I had no place else to turn.

WAITING IN SILENCE

Thwarted & unhappy,
my hungry prayers
crumble like biscuits.

How I covet the holy
concentration of cows,
chomping in silence,
sturdy as ships.

The task of the day —
simple & profound,
learn how to pray.

THE VISION

To step outside
          the rigidity of one's faith
however briefly,
          to see it as if for the
first time, un-besmirched
          in the endless calm
of its simple presence,
          stripped of all its faults
and failures, the terrors,
          rages and doubts of
our onrushing, confused lives —

is a vision that
          reawakens our hunger
for the peaceable kingdom
          lost now in the folds of
memory, keeps us
          yearning to be reclaimed
by its ancient promises.

MYSTERY OF THE WAY

Maybe we're not so bereft or
isolated as we believe — lost
creatures in

the slanted rain of a slippery-
slick world; maybe in the
last days when

the lid of cloud lifts we'll
discover we've been kindred
wayfarers all along

walking a shadowy path strewn
with hints & traces of love,
safe as a bird

nesting in a loving hand beneath
the sweetening sun, close to
the loft of heaven.

LAST WISH

I'd turn to the icon of St. Francis on my
Chamber's wall, pray for a smidgen of his

gentleness to find its way into our legal
world. Going to court would signal a new

direction: no more mulish posturing or
stagy rhetoric, an end to dithering and

legalese. I'd applaud litigants who announce
a truce and shake hands, lawyers who

mastered the art of listening and know
when to hold their tongues. And whenever

I find myself in error, mean-spirited or
smitten by self-importance, I'd call a

recess, gaze at the icon of St. Francis with
a contrite heart, halt my haughty ways.

THE RACE TO PARADISE

Before God created
               man
She took
               a chunk of coal
from the coalbin
and scratched
               a thin line
across the void,
               counted off
seven days
               and seven nights,
and hurled a star
               against
the sky
               (O what a bang!)
               to announce
the start of
               the race to paradise.
That's when men
               began to murder one another.

NIGHT PRAYER

Come to my rescue, O Holy Spirit.
I'm only a man under sentence of

death, tired of chasing the presence
of divinity in the flesh, spinning

utopias in my mind. I need a visible
sign, someone to assure me that

when I pierce the thin lining of this
world You will be there to catch

my perishing breath, decode the
riddle of our fleeting and misshapen

lives. Like the faithful father in
the parable who hosted a party,

roasted the fatted calf, uncorked
the best wine for the errant son,

someone to welcome me home from
the dead, light a flame above my head.

FLAWED MASTER

Keeper of the holy order of things;
master of jurisprudence;
explainer of the changing rules that keep us
safe & fit for human habitation save
the ones that never change & confound us most,

rules that tell us what to live for.

KINDRED SPIRITS

The Virgin & Buddha
would make a fine couple,
they've so much in common,
their differences are subtle.

The Virgin lives in a bathtub
of rocks; the Buddha reclines
on a dais of gold; yet
they're always the same, never
grow old &
neither wears socks.

The Virgin stays out in all kinds
of weather, but never
gets wet; her clothes are
immaculate. The Buddha

nibbles on lichee & rice,
keeps his eyes closed,
& neither is prone to arthritis
or vice.

Their heads are so groovy with
celestial thought, no one
would say they are funny;
the Virgin spends all her

time adoring her Son while
Buddha just squats
on his tummy.

I love the Virgin,
I love the Buddha,
I wish we were friends &
could go to the movies together.

THE LONG WAIT

Consider this:
when he loses heart over the
feeble facsimiles of justice he metes
out in court each day — his inability to
reshape the world and its warped ways —
the old judge retreats to a quiet place
in the country to contemplate in
silence his defeats, the things he would
but cannot change.

All he can do:
gaze across empty fields and pray,
ask God to prove He still exists.
Afraid he won't answer.

SHORT WINTER PRAYER

Death grips the earth in its ice-cold
fist; under a silvery sun, trees glint
naked, — all arthritic knobs & limbs.
This is the zero hour, only a few tattered
leaves remain from last summer's green
towers. Forgive my frailty & unfaith-
fullness O Divine Rescuer, my hope &
salvation. Hasten with the speed of love to
touch my heart with the mercy of spring's
long moist tendrils.

WHITMAN'S HEAVEN

It's been a long, gray winter; spring
inches forward here, but the crocuses

have not poked through & the garden's
damp & dark. Much has changed since

your last visit. I feel lonely & sick at
heart; age is catching up with me. Last

summer when you were here we talked
about heaven. After we die, you said,

we'll float between two worlds till
everyone we love is safe. Pained by

the same dumb desire I wait for
heaven's quick'ning fire to warm my

days, make my flowers grow. I won't let
go till I rest on leaves of grass.

A KIND OF SERMON

If what is said is true & the
Lord we pray to never sleeps,
keeps us safe from toppling over
the brink — relax.

Let your brain curl inside
its shell, forget your doubts;
little blessings will always allay
your fears.

GOING HOME

Be patient.
We are going home.
It is not far. We are rocking
in the great belly of the ship.
No light cracks the dark sea, but
the ship is strong, the voyage
will not be long.

We will arrive early.
It will be morning. We will
rub our unshelled eyes, see
the shore rise.
We will untangle our bones & play
in the lemon groves, dwell
in a white house near blue water.
There will be time. Be patient.
We are going home.

GEOMETRY OF LOVE

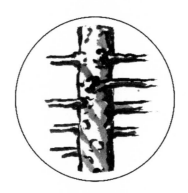

UNENDING LOVE SONG

On my journey to you, love, I stopped to watch light's
little knives carve a single drop of water into glassy
slivers, saw the loose ends of my life split and slide
down silvery slides till sharp reflections mirrored shut
my eyes.

I realize now that passions are never-
ending, the gift of single-heartedness not mine to give.
With interruptions like these it will take me years of
nights to reach you.

ROSES

The man who steps out
of the flower shop into

the gathering dusk, a
bouquet of roses clutched

in his awkward hands
is someone who has

travelled far, knows
what it's like to wear

a blindfold round his
heart, live in a clock-

driven world forgetful
of small kindnesses.

Though chastened by his
blindness, he is not lost.

He's a man on a mission,
thinking of someone

dear, determined to raise
tenderness from its squalor

of neglect, swim against
the past's cold current.

His roses shine in the dark.

THE UNSPEAKABLE SADNESS OF ANGELS

In the beginning there were only the two of them. Those
angels who preside over the dreaming human spirit, shuddered
with delight on their cloudy perches high above the stream as
the woman draped herself across the centre thwart, leaned
back & grasped the gunwhales, while the man crept up from
the stern on hand & knee to begin the awkward ecstasy.

When the canoe tipped tossing the couple into the cold
water the angels at first chuckled. But as eons yawned & fell
back & more & more earthlings were swept away by the
current it slowly dawned on their exotic minds that despite
their unappeasable longing for intimacy, no matter how
closely the man & woman embraced & rubbed against each
other, they could never become one creature, find the still
point that stays the lurch of gravity.

And when the angels observed the man & woman begin to
blame one another for their near-drownings & disappointments
& realized that they would never master the art of lovemaking
in a canoe, that this fault-finding would go on forever, an
unspeakable sadness overtook them & folding their tinselly
wings, they hid their shining faces & wept.

SISYPHUS'S STONE

Day after day,
between morning's spilt coffee &
evening's ragged return

we gather in the vestibule
of the heart
for another lesson
in the hard art
of loving,

which no one
fully masters, but
keeps trying, hoping
to be someday what we aspire
to be next,

tomorrow after tomorrow.

THE CROSSING

She waited on the dock for the ferry
to the outer isles, a man beside her —

companion or lover I couldn't say —
with long, wise mien, and as sea

roiled and licked its green tongue at
dark clouds I felt fearful

— such a rough and perilous crossing —
till I observed the tender way

he gazed at her, the radiance on
her seamless face, as though

skin, eyes, brimmed with inner light,
a hidden sun, and then I knew

she had returned to her beginnings,
the sun-warmed place of giving and

receiving, and was cherished as she'd
always deserved to be, more

than I could ever love, and all
my sadness turned to joy.

AND EVEN IF

it was never meant to be
and she no longer
                 sees me
in the eyes she opens,
I still remember
           once she flew to me,
a goldfinch
           in a darkling wood
singing me home.

And now
           I carve her
in the ivory of my poems,
                    a reflection
in the shady pool,
           an evergreen.

BELOVED

I love the smell of woodsmoke,
the smooth skin of stones,
the shape of a baby's toes;
I loved

                your clear eyes too
where I could see forever,
their gentle "yes" to all;
I won't accept
        they've fallen
            into

                the

                        deep

                              down

                                    blue

beyond my ken.
Love is like death
            only longer.

DESIGNATED DREAMER

...and the dream outlasts
Death, and the dreamer will never die.
— R.S. Thomas

I am your designated dreamer,
intimate like you with the history

of disappointment, steeped in the
shadowlands of sleep, one who

surfs the rag ends of dreams at
night to bring you news of your

buried self, wake you from your
dreamless bed, make you under-

stand there's nothing solid any-
where for you to stand on except

the dark rich earth
of your heart.

FINDING WORDS

Out of the dying embers,
fire-fly sparks
skitter
into the night;

baffled by stirrings
deep within me
of infinite tenderness
for our flickering little light,
I wonder how I'll ever fire into language
the tall starry strangeness
of it all.

ONE HEART

Call it an exchange of
mysteries: it baffles the

foreigner like an idiom; others
skip over words, but

we have learned to marry
our differences, set

them in frames as large
as rooms; not your still

life watercolour, or some-
thing you'll find in the

Oxford dictionary.

And just as doves knit
nests together,

so do we; in love
there is no vacancy.

Outside the cold, inside
the hearth,

and we, one heart,
a green world in it.

EPITHALAMIUM
— for Mira and Bruce

Grown beyond yourselves
      you decide
to share one life, housed
      in one another's arms,
even unto death. Love
      has made you brave.

We, the witnesses,
      mindful of our defections,
long to cry out:
      The journey is too hard,
but deep within us,
      some grace
stirred by fresh beginnings
      sweeps aside our cowardice,
brims our hearts to sweet excess,
      till at last
we dare to sing:
      "Yes, O Yes."

LONG VOYAGE

Today we sit
in the sunroom
whispering small
inconsequential things.

We barely touch
across the deep void
of silence.

Now dark seeps
inside the trees
behind the park,
we watch the sky break

into crimson fires.
I close my eyes, see
us together
in that time

we once entered
that now abandons us,
a world that
would not let us stay.

UNTITLED

There's something I neglected to say
That came to me clear from the blue,
We need love, not bread, for our way.

Cold and brutish the day
When sun is hidden from view.
There's something I neglected to say.

Though marvellously fashioned from clay
We are chippy as chimps in a zoo.
We need love, not bread for our way.

Loyalties will often betray
And vanish like sparks in a flue.
There's something I neglected to say.

Malice can wrench us astray,
We are sheep who gambol on cue.
We need love, not bread, for our way.

Did I tell you this morning I love you?
And need you more than I knew.
These are words I neglected to say,
We need love, not bread, for our way.

HOW AWESOME THE SNOW
— *for Kathy*

After a night of softly
        sifting snow
too fine for
        the net of words,
the kind that
        changes the colour
of your mind by morning,
        I awake to a new
creation safe
        in your loving arms,
venture outside,
        a canticle of whiteness
underfoot, knowing
        I've entered the winter
palace of the heart,
        found peace at last.

A BLESSING

May the winds stirring outside
your window, enter your breath-
filling body, carry you like a new
bird coming to flight into the clean
sunlit air of mountains beyond the
reach of fear, where you can kiss the
sky knowing it will love you back,
your body warms with trust & you
can fly forever.

ABOUT THE AUTHOR

James Clarke is the author of almost twenty books of poetry and memoir, in-
cluding *Dreamworks, Forced Passage, How to Bribe a Judge, L'Arche Journal, A
Mourner's Kaddish, The Raggedy Parade, Silver Mercies,* and *The Way Everyone
is Inside.* He is a former Superior Court judge, and his judgments have been
published extensively in legal journals. He lives in Guelph, Ontario.